The Wackiest Word Game

by Barbara A. Donovan
illustrated by Jim Gordon

Harcourt
SCHOOL PUBLISHERS

Printed in Mexico

ISBN 10: 0-15-351672-0
ISBN 13: 978-0-15-351672-6

Ordering Options
ISBN 10: 0-15-351215-6 (Grade 5 Advanced Collection)
ISBN 13: 978-0-15-351215-5 (Grade 5 Advanced Collection)
ISBN 10: 0-15-358155-7 (package of 5)
ISBN 13: 978-0-15-358155-7 (package of 5)

3 4 5 6 7 8 9 10   126   12 11 10 09 08

Sarah: Welcome to *The Wackiest Word Game.* I'm Sarah, and I'm one of your hosts today. This is William, my cohost.

William: Hi! Let's meet today's players. Our first player is our returning champion, Bobby. At the end of our last show, you got a bit boisterous, Bobby. Tell the audience why.

Bobby: I was playing against a very tough competitor. We were neck and neck all the way until the very last question. When I heard her final sentence, I thought for sure that I had lost the game. I couldn't believe it when the audience voted for my answer over hers. I just went wild. All of the scholarship money I won will really come in handy in a few years. I'm planning to attend a prestigious college, and I'm already saving my money for it.

Sarah: Good for you! Now let's meet Maria, who will be playing against you today. Maria, give us some insight into your life.

Maria: Hi, I attend King Elementary School. I just won my school's Inventor's Fair. My winning invention is called "The Lunch Buddy."

Sarah: What does "The Lunch Buddy" do?

Maria: "The Lunch Buddy" is like a portable kitchen. With it, you can bring both hot and cold food to school. It has one side that stays hot for eight hours. The other side keeps your milk or water cold. You can keep delicious, gourmet lunches at just the right temperature. "The Lunch Buddy" is light enough to carry in your backpack. It's practical for any kid's lunch.

Sarah: Your invention could be useful for picnics, too! Anyway, I propose that we go over the rules of *The Wackiest Word Game*. I will say a word and correctly use it in a sentence. You will each add a hyphen or two somewhere in the word to make a new wacky word that you will use in a wacky sentence or two. Be careful, though. If your wacky word is pronounced differently from the original word, you lose twenty points. Do you understand?

Narrator: Maria and Bobby both nod that they understand.

Sarah: Good! Remember that the winner of the first round gets to play for extra points and cash in the bonus round. Now let's play *The Wackiest Word Game*. The first word for today is measly.

Narrator: The word *measly* appears on a large screen on the wall facing the contestants.

William: The sentence is: *My measly salary is so small that I can barely afford to buy gum.*

Narrator: Both contestants write on the electronic pads in front of them.

Sarah: Bobby, let's reveal your sentence first.

Narrator: Bobby's sentence appears on the large screen. It reads, *I have the measles, so I feel* measl-y.

William: That's very clever! You played on the word *measles* to get a wacky meaning for *measly*. Let's see what Maria wrote.

Narrator: Maria's sentences read: *I use a lot of* me's *in my writing. I'm too* meas-ly.

Sarah: I like that! That's quite a feat. Let's see what the audience thinks. Audience, it's time to vote. Who came up with the wackier word—Bobby or Maria?

Narrator: The audience members punch their votes into electronic devices that protrude from the arms of their chairs. As each vote is punched in, it is added to a tally on the large screen. At last, the final vote is cast.

William: This was a tough choice. Bobby received 286 votes, and Maria received 114 votes. Bobby, you are the winner of this round! Congratulations!

Sarah: Here's the next word. It's *deductions*. The sentence is: *To solve her case, the detective had to make many clever deductions.*

Narrator: Maria starts writing right away. Bobby looks baffled at first. Before long, he starts writing. Maria finishes first. Bobby writes until a buzzer sounds. William calls out that time is up.

William: Maria, what is your wacky word?

Narrator: On the large screen, Maria's sentences appear. They read: *My job is to remove old heating ducts. I do* de-ductions.

Sarah: Great job! You used the prefix *de-* to mean "remove." You have good instincts for this game! Let's see what Bobby wrote.

Narrator: Bobby's sentence appears on the large screen. It says: Deduct-ions *are when ions are removed from atoms.*

William: Let's see how the audience votes. Audience, vote now!

Narrator: The audience members press the appropriate buttons to vote for either Bobby or Maria. The votes appear on the large screen.

Sarah: It looks like Maria is the clear winner of this round. Maria received 351 votes. Bobby only got 49 votes.

William: That's too bad, Bobby. Also, when you say your wacky word, *deduct-ion*, it does not sound the same as the original word. You will lose twenty points for that. Here are your total scores for both rounds. Bobby has 315 votes. Maria has 465 votes.

Narrator: The audience claps and cheers.

William: Let's go on to the next word. It's circulate.

Sarah: Here's the sentence for this word: *When you stir water around in a pot, the water tends to circulate in that same direction even after you take your spoon out of the water.*

Narrator: The word *circulate* appears on the large screen. Both Maria and Bobby glance at the word and start writing. After a minute, both have finished writing.

Sarah: Bobby, what wacky word did you make?

Narrator: Bobby's sentences appear on the screen. They read: *The famous British knight missed his cue while performing on the stage. The person giving the actor his clues whispered, "Cir-cu-late!"* The audience laughs when William reads the sentence aloud.

William: Yes, a knight is called "sir." Very good. Now let's see what Maria wrote.

Narrator: Maria's sentences appear on the large screen: *I might get lost, drive around in circles, and be late to the party. I might* circu-late.

Sarah: Well, that is wacky! Let's see what the audience thinks.

Narrator: The audience votes, and the scores show on the screen. This time Bobby gets 275 votes, and Maria gets 125 votes.

William: The audience is fickle. This time Bobby wins the vote, but look at this! The total scores are Bobby with 590 votes, and Maria with 591 votes! As we go into the final round, they are only separated by one vote! Let's go!

Sarah: The word this time is *equipped*. The sentence is: *The hikers were equipped with tents, sleeping bags, food, water, and other gear.*

Narrator: The word *equipped* appears on the large screen. Bobby, with an irrepressible smile on his face, starts writing. Maria, on the other hand, scours her brain for an idea. Finally, she too begins.

William: Time's up. Let's see what Maria's wacky word is.

Narrator: Maria shakes her head.

Sarah: Oh, I am so sorry, Maria. You did not finish your sentence. If Bobby finished his, he'll get all 400 points and win the game. Let's see what Bobby wrote.

Narrator: Bobby beams as his sentences appear on the large screen. They read: *I e-mailed a joke to my friends. I e-quipped them.*

Sarah: Oh, I get it. To quip is to make a joke! That is wonderful! Congratulations, Bobby! You are the winner again today!

Bobby: Thank you! Thank you!

Narrator: Maria leans over and shakes Bobby's hand. Bobby beams with pleasure at his new score of 990.

William: That 990 points means you have $990 added to the money you have already won. You may have college paid for by the time you get out of elementary school.

Sarah: Bobby, it's time to play your bonus round. Here are three cards. Each one has a hyphen on it. You will have fifteen seconds to place a hyphen in each of the three words we will show you. Then you must use each of your wacky words in a sentence.

William: Our director will decide whether each sentence earns an extra 100 points. If you earn those extra points for each of the three words, then you'll win 200 additional points. That is a total of 500 points for this round. Are you ready?

Bobby: I'm as ready as I'll ever be!

Narrator: A curtain opens to reveal a large frame. Inside the frame are three rows of lighted squares. Each square is suspended between a top and a bottom wire. This lets the player slide the letters from side to side. The player must place a hyphen between two letters in each word.

Sarah: Bobby is ready! Let's see today's bonus words.

Narrator: Letters appear on the squares on the game board. Three words appear. They are *tempted*, *vetoed*, and *embarked*.

William: Bobby, you have fifteen seconds from . . . now!

Narrator: Bobby rushes up to the board to slide a hyphen in between *p* and *t* in *tempted*. He stares at *vetoed* for a few seconds. Then he moves on to *embarked*. After a few more seconds, he slips a hyphen between the *m* and the *b*. Then he stares at *vetoed* again. Just as time is about to run out, Bobby places a hyphen between the *e* and the *t*. A buzzer sounds to end the round.

Sarah: Wow! You just made it, Bobby. Let's see if your wacky words will earn you any bonus points, and possibly the 200-point super bonus for scoring 100 points on all three. The first word is *tempted*. What's your wacky sentence?

Bobby: *My name is Ted, and I work for a temporary agency. I'm* Temp-Ted.

Narrator: The scoreboard lights up and displays the number 100.

William: Congratulations, Bobby, you've just earned an extra 100 points. Now let's hear your second sentence. You hesitated a bit before this one. Do you think you have a winner?

Bobby: I believe I do. *The scientist discovered an animal that has only two toes that are joined together at their base to form a* V. *They have discovered a* ve-toed *animal.*

Narrator: Everyone laughs at Bobby's sentence, and the scoreboard shows that another 100 has been added to Bobby's score.

Sarah: It's time for your final word. How well did you do?

Bobby: I'm not sure, but here it is. *My dog is named Emma, but I call her "Em." When a stranger came to our house,* Em-barked.

Narrator: The audience claps at Bobby's wacky word. They cheer as another 100 shows on the scoreboard. Then two more 100s appear to give Bobby a total of 500 points for the bonus round. Bobby's score changes to 1,490. Bobby begins jumping up and down and cheering when he sees his new score.

Sarah: Congratulations to our continuing champion, Bobby! He earned 500 points during the bonus round to bring his point total for two days to 2,685. Unfortunately, that's all the time we have today to play *The Wackiest Word Game.* Tune in tomorrow when we'll find out if Bobby can continue his winning streak.

Narrator: A throng of people gathers to congratulate Bobby.

William: Ooh, it's an invasion of Bobby's family and friends! Good-bye for now from all of us at *The Wackiest Word Game!*

Think Critically

1. What skills does a player need to win at *The Wackiest Word Game*?

2. Do you think the game's scoring system is fair? Why or why not?

3. Would you like to be a contestant on *The Wackiest Word Game*? Explain why or why not.

4. Why is the Narrator's role an important one in this Readers' Theater?

5. How is *The Wackiest Word Game* like other game shows you know? How is it different?

 Language Arts

Make Wacky Words Scan your vocabulary list or reading book for words to use to make wacky words. Write each word, and add one or two hyphens in the middle. Then write a sentence or two to show what the wacky word means.

 School-Home Connection Explain to a family member how to play *The Wackiest Word Game*. Then explain why Bobby's and Maria's wacky words did or did not work.

Word Count: 1,868